Francis Frith's
Norfolk

Photographic Memories

Francis Frith's
Norfolk

Revised edition of original work by

Terence Sackett

First published in the United Kingdom in 1998
by WBC Ltd

Revised paperback edition published in the United Kingdom in 2000
by Frith Book Company Ltd
ISBN 1-85937-195-7

Reprinted in paperback 2001

British Library Cataloguing in Publication Data

Francis Frith's Norfolk
Terence Sackett

Frith Book Company Ltd
Frith's Barn, Teffont,
Salisbury, Wiltshire SP3 5QP
Tel: +44 (0) 1722 716 376
Email: info@francisfrith.co.uk
www.francisfrith.co.uk

Printed and bound in Great Britain

Front Cover: Hoveton 1921 70890

Contents

Francis Frith: *Victorian Pioneer*

FRANCIS FRITH, Victorian founder of the world-famous photographic archive, was a complex and multitudinous man. A devout Quaker and a highly successful Victorian businessman, he was both philosophic by nature and pioneering in outlook.

By 1855 Francis Frith had already established a wholesale grocery business in Liverpool, and sold it for the astonishing sum of £200,000, which is the equivalent today of over £15,000,000. Now a multi-millionaire, he was able to indulge his passion for travel. As a child he had pored over travel books written by early explorers, and his fancy and imagination had been stirred by family holidays to the sublime mountain regions of Wales and Scotland. 'What a land of spirit-stirring and enriching scenes and places!' he had written. He was to return to these scenes of grandeur in later years to 'recapture the thousands of vivid and tender memories', but with a different purpose. Now in his thirties, and captivated by the new science of photography, Frith set out on a series of pioneering journeys to the Nile regions that occupied him from 1856 until 1860.

Intrigue and Adventure

He took with him on his travels a specially-designed wicker carriage that acted as both dark-room and sleeping chamber. These far-flung journeys were packed with intrigue and adventure. In his life story, written when he was sixty-three, Frith tells of being held captive by bandits, and of fighting 'an awful midnight battle to the very point of surrender with a deadly pack of hungry, wild dogs'. Sporting flowing Arab costume, Frith arrived at Akaba by camel seventy years before Lawrence, where he encountered 'desert princes and rival sheikhs, blazing with jewel-hilted swords'.

During these extraordinary adventures he was assiduously exploring the desert regions bordering the Nile and patiently recording the antiquities and peoples with his camera. He was the first photographer to venture beyond the sixth cataract. Africa was still the mysterious 'Dark Continent', and Stanley and Livingstone's historic meeting was a decade into the future. The conditions for picture taking confound belief. He laboured for hours in his wicker dark-room in the sweltering heat of the desert, while the volatile chemicals fizzed dangerously in their trays. Often he was forced to work in remote tombs and caves where conditions were cooler. Back in London he exhibited his photographs and was 'rapturously cheered' by members of the Royal Society. His reputation as a photographer was made overnight. An eminent modern historian has likened their impact on the population of the time to that on our own generation of the first photographs taken on the surface of the moon.

Venture of a Life-Time

Characteristically, Frith quickly spotted the opportunity to create a new business as a specialist publisher of photographs. He lived in an era of immense and sometimes violent change. For the poor in the early part of Victoria's reign work was a drudge and the hours long, and people had precious little free time to enjoy themselves. Most had no transport other than a cart or gig at their disposal, and had not travelled far beyond the

boundaries of their own town or village. However, by the 1870s, the railways had threaded their way across the country, and Bank Holidays and half-day Saturdays had been made obligatory by Act of Parliament. All of a sudden the ordinary working man and his family were able to enjoy days out and see a little more of the world.

With characteristic business acumen, Francis Frith foresaw that these new tourists would enjoy having souvenirs to commemorate their days out. In 1860 he married Mary Ann Rosling and set out with the intention of photographing every city, town and village in Britain. For the next thirty years he travelled the country by train and by pony and trap, producing fine photographs of seaside resorts and beauty spots that were keenly bought by millions of Victorians. These prints were painstakingly pasted into family albums and pored over during the dark nights of winter, rekindling precious memories of summer excursions.

The Rise of Frith & Co

Frith's studio was soon supplying retail shops all over the country. To meet the demand he gathered about him a small team of photographers, and published the work of independent artist-photographers of the calibre of Roger Fenton and Francis Bedford. In order to gain some understanding of the scale of Frith's business one only has to look at the catalogue issued by Frith & Co in 1886: it runs to some 670 pages, listing not only many thousands of views of the British Isles but also many photographs of most European countries, and China, Japan, the USA and

Canada – note the sample page shown above from the hand-written *Frith & Co* ledgers detailing pictures taken. By 1890 Frith had created the greatest specialist photographic publishing company in the world, with over 2,000 outlets – more than the combined number that Boots and W H Smith have today! The picture on the right shows the *Frith & Co* display board at Ingleton in the Yorkshire Dales. Beautifully constructed with mahogany frame and gilt inserts, it could display up to a dozen local scenes.

Postcard Bonanza

The ever-popular holiday postcard we know today took many years to develop. In 1870 the Post Office issued the first plain cards, with a pre-printed stamp on one face. In 1894 they allowed other publishers' cards to be sent through the mail with an attached adhesive halfpenny stamp. Demand grew rapidly, and in 1895 a new size of postcard was permitted called the court card, but there was little room for illustration. In 1899, a year after Frith's death, a new card measuring 5.5 x 3.5 inches became the standard format, but it was not until 1902 that the divided back came into being, with address and message on one face and a full-size illustration on the other. *Frith & Co* were in the vanguard of postcard development, and Frith's sons Eustace and Cyril continued their father's monumental task, expanding the number of views offered to the public and recording more and more places in Britain, as the coasts and countryside were opened up to mass travel.

Francis Frith died in 1898 at his villa in Cannes, his great project still growing. The archive he created continued in business for another seventy years. By 1970 it contained over a third of a million pictures of 7,000 cities, towns and villages. The massive photographic record Frith has left to us stands as a living monument to a special and very remarkable man.

Frith's Archive: *A Unique Legacy*

FRANCIS FRITH'S legacy to us today is of immense significance and value, for the magnificent archive of evocative photographs he created provides a unique record of change in 7,000 cities, towns and villages throughout Britain over a century and more. Frith and his fellow studio photographers revisited locations many times down the years to update their views, compiling for us an enthralling and colourful pageant of British life and character.

We tend to think of Frith's sepia views of Britain as nostalgic, for most of us use them to conjure up memories of places in our own lives with which we have family associations. It often makes us forget that to Francis Frith they were records of daily life as it was actually being lived in the cities, towns and villages of his day. The Victorian age was one of great and often bewildering change for ordinary people, and though the pictures evoke an impression of slower times, life was as busy and hectic as it is today.

We are fortunate that Frith was a photographer of the people, dedicated to recording the minutiae of everyday life. For it is this sheer wealth of visual data, the painstaking chronicle of changes in dress, transport, street layouts, buildings, housing, engineering and landscape that captivates us so much today. His remarkable images offer us a powerful link with the past and with the lives of our ancestors.

Today's Technology

Computers have now made it possible for Frith's many thousands of images to be accessed almost instantly. In the Frith archive today, each photograph is carefully 'digitised' then stored on a CD Rom. Frith archivists can locate a single photograph amongst thousands within seconds. Views can be catalogued and sorted under a variety of categories of place and content to the immediate benefit of researchers.

Inexpensive reference prints can be created for them at the touch of a mouse button, and a wide range of books and other printed materials assembled and published for a wider, more general readership - in the next twelve months over a hundred Frith local history titles will be published! The day-to-day workings of the archive are very different from how they were in Francis Frith's time: imagine the herculean task of sorting through eleven tons of glass negatives as Frith had to do to locate a particular

THE FRANCIS FRITH COLLECTION
Photographic publishers since 1860

HOME | PHOTO SEARCH | BOOKS | PORTFOLIO | GALLERY   MY CART
Products | History | Other Collections | Contact us | Help?

your town,
your village

365,000
photographs of 7,000 towns and villages, taken between 1860 & 1970.

The Frith Archive
The Frith Archive is the remarkable legacy of its energetic and visionary founder. Today, the Frith archive is the only nationally important archive of its kind still in private ownership.

The Collection is world-renowned for the extraordinary quality of its images.

The Gallery
This month The Frith Gallery features images from "Frith's Egypt".

News...
Image update complete.
An additional 5,000 images have been added and the quality of all images has now been improved.

Sample Chapters avaiable.
The first selection of sample chapters from the Frith Book Co.'s extensive range is now available. All are offered in Pdf format for easy downloading and viewing.

explore
FRITH
Search thousands of photographs from one of the worlds' great archives.

Town search
[   ] GO

County search
[Select a county ▾] GO

the FRITHgallery

See Frith at www.francisfrith.co.uk

sequence of pictures! Yet the archive still prides itself on maintaining the same high standards of excellence laid down by Francis Frith, including the painstaking cataloguing and indexing of every view.

It is curious to reflect on how the internet now allows researchers in America and elsewhere greater instant access to the archive than Frith himself ever enjoyed. Many thousands of individual views can be called up on screen within seconds on one of the Frith internet sites, enabling people living continents away to revisit the streets of their ancestral home town, or view places in Britain where they have enjoyed holidays. Many overseas researchers welcome the chance to view special theme selections, such as transport, sports, costume and ancient monuments.

We are certain that Francis Frith would have heartily approved of these modern developments in imaging techniques, for he himself was always working at the very limits of Victorian photographic technology.

The Value of the Archive Today

Because of the benefits brought by the computer, Frith's images are increasingly studied by social historians, by researchers into genealogy and ancestory, by architects, town planners, and by teachers and schoolchildren involved in local history projects.

In addition, the archive offers every one of us an opportunity to examine the places where we and our families have lived and worked down the years. Highly successful in Frith's own era, the archive is now, a century and more on, entering a new phase of popularity.

The Past in Tune with the Future

Historians consider the Francis Frith Collection to be of prime national importance. It is the only archive of its kind remaining in private ownership and has been valued at a million pounds. However, this figure is now rapidly increasing as digital technology enables more and more people around the world to enjoy its benefits.

Francis Frith's archive is now housed in an historic timber barn in the beautiful village of Teffont in Wiltshire. Its founder would not recognize the archive office as it is today. In place of the many thousands of dusty boxes containing glass plate negatives and an all-pervading odour of photographic chemicals, there are now ranks of computer screens. He would be amazed to watch his images travelling round the world at unimaginable speeds through network and internet lines.

The archive's future is both bright and exciting. Francis Frith, with his unshakeable belief in making photographs available to the greatest number of people, would undoubtedly approve of what is being done today with his lifetime's work. His photographs, depicting our shared past, are now bringing pleasure and enlightenment to millions around the world a century and more after his death.

Norfolk - *An Introduction*

Norfolk is made up of two distinct regions. Its first is a varied region of bare sandy heathlands in the west, marshlands and reedbeds in the east, and broad agricultural lands between, rolling along under expansive skies and studded with remote and picturesque villages. Its second more celebrated region is to be found at its margins, where a hundred miles of wind-blown coastline are swept by the relentless waves of the North Sea.

Though entirely separate in nature and character, these two countries are intimately joined by Norfolk's willow-fringed rivers, such as the Yare, Wensum and Thurne, which thread their way through its broad landscapes and wind past remote farms and villages. Through the county's long history these waterways have been vital carriers of agricultural produce and other goods for export to markets in Britain and

overseas, and have opened the county up to the wider world.

Norfolk has a rich seafaring heritage. Since medieval times, its great harbours at King's Lynn and Yarmouth have been the haunt of fishermen following the herring and gathering the plentiful lobsters and shellfish in its quieter coastal waters. For many hundreds of years coastal trading vessels have wound their way down the county's waterways to offload freights from the Low Countries. Many of Norfolk's ancient ports have long since silted-up and have discovered new roles as popular resort towns. Cromer, Sheringham, Wells and Hunstanton are now thronged with visitors in the summer months. Behind their crumbling cliffs are wide, solitary marshes, some now drained and cultivated, and rich in bird life.

Norfolk has been shaped to its core by the

sea. For centuries, men have exercised their ingenuity in fending off the encroaching waters and reclaiming their fields and pastures. Where the dunes have been breached by tides the seas have flooded in. The old windmills that speckle Norfolk's rich, black marshlands, and the complex networks of dykes, bear testament to man's continual battle with nature. At the heart of the county are the Broads, unique shallow lagoons, shaped by the hands of medieval peat diggers, now the pleasure grounds of the county and the exclusive province of holiday and leisure craft.

Although it is a county of sparse population, Norfolk's towns and villages are rich in fine old buildings. The streets and market places of its market towns like East Dereham, Swaffham and Thetford reveal a pleasing harmony of flint and brick. King's Lynn, close by the Wash, is a treasure house of architectural gems. Norfolk's crowning glory, however, is the city of Norwich with its magnificent cathedral and winding streets of jettied houses.

Much of Norfolk has avoided the mechanisation found in other regions of Britain. It is still a county where the visitor can enjoy peace and solitude. It has long been a painter's paradise. Cotman and Crome have brought it renown, finding inspiration there for their celebrated water-colours, and transmuting its soft, liquid landscape tones into paint. Norfolk is a county that can still conjure the spirit of another age, away from the bustle and noise of the modern world.

Norwich, Pulls Ferry 1891 28157
By the banks of the graceful River Wensum is the 15th-century gateway to the city's diminutive canal, which penetrates its way to the margins of the cathedral. Along this waterway medieval bargeman hauled the Caen stone used in the construction of the lofty spire and vaults. The watergate was restored in the late 1940s.

Norwich & Inland

There is a spacious air about Norwich, the capital of Norfolk and 'city of churches'. At its heart are a great cattle market and two magnificent buildings, the cathedral and the castle, both Norman in origin. Parts of its old medieval walls are still standing and this deepens its atmosphere of history and tradition.

Left: **Norwich, Market Place 1891** 29133
This broad open space is a kaleidoscope of noise and colour on market day. In the background is the soaring tower of the 15th-century 180ft long church of St Peter Mancroft, with its peal of twelve bells and concealed hammerbeam roof. Below it a huge hoarding is smothered with trade notices - the Victorians were as keen as businessmen are today to shout their slogans and announcements. The buildings to the right of the church were demolished in the 1930s and the market extended. Note the pencil outlining on the church - a device used by the Frith re-touchers in the creation of artworks for postcards. Here it looks more than a little crude.

Below: **Norwich, Market Place 1929** 81796
Although motor cars have replaced the horses and carts, this 1929 view of the ancient Provision Market is, in essence, little changed from medieval days. The cries of the traders still echo above the sea of bright awnings, and handcarts still ply their trade amidst the throng.

Norwich, The Royal Hotel & Post Office 1901 46672
This busy prospect reveals the pleasing mix of architectural styles inevitable in any prosperous city.
On the right is the old post office and the agricultural hall. Opposite is the Royal Hotel, with its red brick facade, steep roofs and decorative towers, promising the Victorian traveller a sophisticated welcome.

Norwich, Davey Place 1922 72602

This tiny street of small shops offers a glimpse of the city's gleaming white castle, which rises from a great mound raised in prehistoric times. Until the 19th century the castle keep was in use as a prison. The narrow passage was built in the early 19th century to link the market at the castle with the central market place.

Norwich, Elm Hill 1929 81805
This winding cobbled street, edged with handsome medieval timber-framed houses with flint-faced ground floors, was anciently known as Houndgate. A fire destroyed many of its buildings in 1507. It is extraordinary to think that it was scheduled for demolition earlier this century.

Norwich, The Guildhall 1891 28164
This beautiful 15th-century building overlooks the market place. From here the city has been governed since 1407. The glorious east-end, with its decorative chequerwork detailing, was completed in 1535. The structure was once almost undermined by saltpetre diggers.

Norwich, Ber Street 1891 28162
Ber Street leads the traveller out through the southern fringes of the city. This quiet, shaded street offered a little respite from the bustle of the market centre. The jumble of roof lines reveals how city streets often developed piecemeal. On the right is a fine display of baskets and tinware, although the street was known at one time for its slaughter houses.

Norwich, Old Cow Tower 1891 28158
This massive medieval structure, formed of flint and ruddy Dutch bricks, squats close by the river, near Bishop Bridge. No one now knows why it was called 'Cow Tower', for in previous days it was the water toll gate where the monks' servants collected taxes on vessels plying the river.

Norwich, The River Wensum 1896 37364

Traversed by a dozen bridges, the Wensum clutches the old city in a tight embrace. It was once a vital waterway for the carrying of fleeces and woollen produce, for Norwich was once one of the great weaving centres of medieval England.

Thorpe-Next-Norwich, On the River 1919 69075
John Sell Cotman, who founded the Norwich School of Artists with Crome, was born in this riverside village in 1782. The banks of the Yare are thick with chestnuts and willows, and pleasure boats and dinghies glide through smooth waters between fine old houses. Thorpe is now almost a suburb of Norwich. Further down is the Rush Cutters pub.

◄ **Wymondham, The Green Dragon c1965** W159027
This exquisite old timbered inn once belonged to the priory. Its jettied upper storey projects out over the latticed windows below. It is a tragedy of our century that the elevations of many of our finest buildings are defaced by the necessities of modern life. If only Mr Bird could have sited his garage elsewhere!

◀ Wymondham, Market Place & Cross c1965

W159036

This pleasant market town sits on the road from Thetford to Norwich, and was once a resting place for pilgrims - it still has a fine Guild Chapel dedicated to St Thomas a Becket. The town is renowned for the number and quality of its historic houses, and is blessed with an ancient abbey, founded by William d'Albini in 1107. The half-timbered octagonal market cross, resting on timber stilts and stone arches, was built in 1605 after a fire destroyed a good proportion of the town. It has an outside wooden stair leading to a reading room. Crowning the imposing pyramid roof is a weathercock.

▼ East Dereham, Church Street 1893 33303

This lovely street, fringed with cobbles, leads down to the White Lion Inn and the old church, where the poet William Cowper, 'England's sweetest and most pious bard', was laid to rest. On the left is Kerrison the butcher's ornamented shop front, with a refined iron balcony overhead.

◀ East Dereham The Town Sign c1955

D163100

The Victorians were renowned for commemorating civic occasions in public architecture. In 1954, in similar fashion, the citizens of the town erected this imposing frieze across the roofs in memory of Withburga, daughter of one of the kings of the East Anglians. She established a nunnery at Dereham, and was laid to rest here in 654.

East Dereham 1893
33308
A quiet lane on the fringes of the town. Washing dries in the breeze in the gardens of plain, mellow cottages. In the background are the two towers of St Nicholas's church - the second detached bell tower was built in the churchyard in the 15th century. It has a Norman south doorway and a celebrated panelled font of 1468 which cost £12 13s 9d.

'On the evening of July, in the year 18-, at East D-, a beautiful little town in a certain district of East Anglia, I first saw the light.' George Borrow, the 'gentleman gypsy', was lucky to have been born in this pleasing old country town. It enjoys a prosperity founded on more than its market and agricultural traditions. Engineering works were established here in Victorian times and Dereham grew into one of the busiest centres of commerce in central Norfolk.

◀ **Fakenham, Market Square 1929** 82020 Some splendid Georgian brick buildings surround Fakenham's square. Eighteenth-century architects, usually local men, worked from standard pattern books, yet managed to achieve townscapes of individual character and harmony.

◀ **Fakenham, Norwich Street c1955** F3002
Norwich Street reflects Fakenham's essential character. None of its brick buildings is outstanding yet the total effect is one of pleasing harmony. Many of the shops have retained their Victorian detailing. The postman is delivering from his two-wheeled basket cart.

▼ **Castle Acre, The Old Gate 1891** 29111
Spanning the narrow street of this hill-top village, which rests high on the chalk uplands overlooking the River Nar, is this monumental arch, ancient gateway to the castle, which lies ruinous close by. Though castle and gateway were Norman-built, the settlement's origins are still more ancient, for it stands on the line of the Peddar Way, an ancient Celtic track.

◀ **Swaffham, Market Place 1891** 29104
This admirable market town, with its Queen Anne and Georgian buildings, was once hailed as 'the Montpellier of England'. Five roads meet at the market square. All around is a medley of harmonious red-brick. The church of St Peter and St Paul is a magnificent Perpendicular edifice with a grand hammerbeam roof and delicate spire.

Diss and the South

Diss, this small, stylish town on the Suffolk border evolved around a six-acre pool called Diss Mere which penetrates almost to the edge of the main street. The town prospered in medieval times as a market for cloth and linen thread, which was spun and woven from local flax. The poet John Skelton was rector here for a quarter of a century.

Diss, Market Place 1925 77322
The spacious market place is dominated by the venerable flint church of St Mary's with its Norman tower, 14th-century arcades, impressive clerestory, and knapped flint chancel. The Company of Change Ringers still ring out a traditional peal on the fine bells. In front of the church are the single-storied Shambles, fronted by an open stone-columned arcade. It was once busy with butchers' cries.

Diss, Market Place c1965 D32033
In this later view very little seems to have changed. The delightful medley of building styles creates a harmonious prospect along the street. On the left is 'The King's Head', its signboard depicting Henry VIII - John Skelton was tutor to the portly King when he was still Prince of Wales.

Diss, Mere Street 1925 77324
This view shows the foot of Mere Street, close by Diss Mere. On the left is West's Garage, offering Shell petrol and BP car batteries. Only decades before, there would have been a bustling scene of drovers and animals pressing a noisy path through the narrow street to the market.

Diss, Mere Street 1925 77325
Mere Street funnels its way, tight as a shirt collar, to the market place. Above the doorway of the shop on the right is the famous logo of 'His Master's Voice' - the gramophone had become a fashionable gadget in every home.

Garboldisham, The Post Office c1955 G188031
Mr Burden's shop and Post Office is the centre of village life. Here we see the local bobby returning to his beat - his cycle is parked under the signpost. On the wall is a bubble gum machine, once a popular feature of the frontage of every village store in the country. At the southern limits of the county, close by Diss, this delightful village of knapped flint cottages sits in wooded countryside in the valley of the Little Ouse.

Garboldisham, Harvest Time c1955 G188029
This photograph depicts a vanished way of life in the country. Horse-drawn wagons have brought in the straw from the fields. The rick-maker is at work - you can just spot a conical thatched roof in the background. Within a decade or two the roar of the combines would replace the peaceful scene.

Thetford, St Cuthbert's Church 1921 70915
St Cuthbert's is a medieval church that was entirely rebuilt after its tower fell in 1851. On the right is the 1884 post office, with its decorative detailing, recalling the ancient East Anglian tradition of pargetting. Thetford enjoyed a high standing a millennium ago - in the 11th century it was the seat of the East Anglian bishopric. However, unlike the more northerly Norfolk towns, it never grew into a major agricultural centre - the soils here are poor.

Thetford, Mill Head 1929 81834
The mill occupies an island between the two rivers, Thet and Little Ouse. In 1669 the course of the Little Ouse was cut and extended to Thetford, enabling barges to ply for the first time between the country towns of the region and the port of King's Lynn. By that date, however, Lynn had already declined in status as a port, and Thetford never gained the prominence as a trading centre it expected.

Thetford, Market Place 1929 81830
In the market place is the Guildhall, rebuilt in 1900. Inside is a splendid collection of a hundred portraits of members of great East Anglian families, which were bequeathed by the antiquary Prince Frederick Duleep Singh. It is market day, and the bystanders are waiting for transport to carry them back to their villages.

Great Yarmouth and the East Coast

This celebrated east coast resort has been a flourishing fishing port since the Conqueror's times. For centuries it suffered continual silting. By the 16th century the old river channel had become so blocked with sandbanks that the town burghers had to enlist the help of Dutch engineers to cut a new river mouth.

Great Yarmouth, The Market Place 1891 28716
The expansive market place has long been the commercial hub of the town. On market days it echoes Yarmouth's seafaring traditions, the colourful awnings stretching out like waves to the horizon. The glory of Yarmouth is its parish church of St Nicholas, the spire soaring high over the distant roofs. It was badly damaged by bombing in the Second World War. Originally a simple Norman construction, it was enlarged many times and given a neo-Gothic interior after the War, with broad aisles. Fortunately, the town still has one fine historic church - St George's was built in 1714 by John Price, and has characteristic 18th-century galleries, pulpit and reredos, and a plaster ceiling above the nave.

▼ **Great Yarmouth, The Market Place 1908** 60651
Farmers' wives and country women have been up since dawn packing their baskets
with jars of home-made jams and marmalades, fresh-picked cabbages and
cucumbers, and journeying in to market day on the carriers' carts. The true market
traders went from town to town attending the markets, livestock sales and hiring
fairs. They had their patch and followed the local farming calendar.

▼ **Great Yarmouth, Town Hall 1891** G56501
The imposing Queen Anne style Town Hall was built in 1882. The buildings
clustering around this broad space, with their balconies, steep roofs and
shutters, reveal a continental influence and reflect the town's cosmopolitan
character - a legacy of its historic trading links with Europe.

▲ **Great Yarmouth
Britannia Pier 1894**
33385
The town rose swiftly to
the challenge of the new
tourism in the Victorian
era. Piers were
constructed and seaside
attractions of all kinds
soon sprang up.
Clustering with other
booths and stalls under
the pier is Wright's
'Noted Tea Saloon'. In the
foreground is a tiny
carriage pulled by a pair
of goats.

◄ **Great Yarmouth, Britannia Pier 1904**

52337

Many seaside piers began life as landing stages for pleasure steamers. Thrusting out into the sea they encapsulated the Victorian passion for exotic feats of engineering. Piers were soon the focus for holiday fun, where visitors could enjoy a concert or simply sit watching the crowds flow by. Britannia Pier was constructed in the mid 19th century, and is 810ft long.

Great Yarmouth, Britannia Pier 1908 60647
This photograph shows the Britannia pier just four years later with a new helter skelter. Hoardings advertise summer seasons by the Brothers Howard and Miss Ruth Vincent. Visitors could also attend a fashionable fancy dress ball.

Great Yarmouth, Wellington Gardens 1904 52338
Wellington Gardens is styled in the classical manner, with a domed bandstand reminiscent of St Paul's. Here the fashionable promenaded. The Winter Gardens to the left have been compared to a giant greenhouse where summer could be enjoyed the year long. The intention was clearly to create a holiday fantasy, worlds away from the grime and slog of city life. Beyond is the mid-Victorian Wellington Pier, since considerably refashioned.

Great Yarmouth, Town Hall 1891 28699
Along Hall Quay are clustered craft of every kind: flat-bottomed barges, wherries and fishing boats - it is still the age of the sail. On the left is a line of coal wagons: Yarmouth had long been a colliers' port, and in the 1700s over 200 vessels were registered.

Great Yarmouth, Quay Bridge 1896 37953
The neighbourhood by the quays is the historic heart of old Yarmouth. Here are the wharves where scores of vessels tied up to unload their catches. Scots fisher girls followed the herring shoals down to the port in the autumn and worked tirelessly day and night gutting and packing.

Great Yarmouth 1887
19860
In this early view of the beach, there are already signs of local businesses capitalising on the new influx of visitors, with terraces of newly-built lodging houses and cheap hotels. A fleet of numbered pleasure craft is grouped on the sands. There are refreshments booths, gingerbread sellers, seats to rent by the hour, and donkey rides.

◄ **Great Yarmouth, Cromwell Hotel 1896**

37952

As Yarmouth blossomed in popularity entire boulevards of hotels were built. A little along from the Town Hall we see the prestigious Cromwell Hotel, embellished with an airy cast iron balcony. To its right is the Commercial Hotel, and further along Steele's and the Crown and Anchor, the latter smothered in creeper.

Great Yarmouth, Regent Road 1896 37959

A peaceful scene away from the bustle of the front. In the hazy distance are the sails of boats. The street is lined with a medley of newly-constructed buildings. Victorian Yarmouth grew out of the efforts of individual speculators, with the consequence that there was no prevailing plan or blueprint to ensure a harmonious townscape, as there would have been in Georgian times.

Great Yarmouth, King's Street 1896 37957

This notable shopping street leads out of the market place towards the river. The awnings are up so it must be a sweltering summer's day. Delivery boys are everywhere, and had to work in rain or shine, dashing between hotels with provisions. Mr Buck the wholesale dealer is calling at St George's Hall, the china and glass emporium.

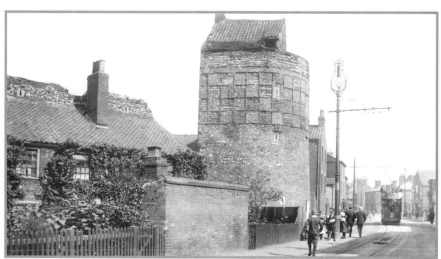

Great Yarmouth, Blackfriars Tower 1908 60653

This well-worn structure of decorative flint work was part of the old medieval town walls, built as a fortification at the end of the 13th century. It was raised in height in the time of the threat of the Spanish Armada. Until the 19th century, building was kept within the old walls. After this date there was an inevitable spreading of streets and tramways.

Great Yarmouth, Row number 60 1908 60654
Huddled around the quay were Yarmouth's famous Rows, close to 140 narrow foot passages. They were likened by Dickens to the bars of a gridiron. Congested with cottages, whitewashed yards and washing lines, they were the home ground of the working population of the town. Most of them were severely damaged by bombing in the war.

Gorleston 1904 52329
In this quintessential holiday scene a pleasure craft hoists its sail ready to carry a party of trippers up and down the coast. Children paddle in the shallows clutching their buckets and spades. In the background is one of Gorleston's many hotels, built to cater for the more well-heeled Edwardian visitor.

Gorleston, The Pier 1904 52331
This solid structure, with its massive piles and defences, hints at the treacherous seas seafarers confronted off the Norfolk coast. An elegant lady shields her pale skin from the sun with a parasol. Beyond her, anglers cast their lines in expectation and a steamer prepares to berth at the quay.

Gorleston, The Sands 1896 37974
A lone tent sits on the empty sands. On the right is a bathing machine, which would be trundled down into the shallows by the patient horse so that lady bathers could dip their toes with no fear of prying eyes. Gorleston stands at the gateway of Yarmouth's harbour overlooking the River Yare and the sea. It had long been an old seafaring port but burgeoned into a sizeable town in the 19th century. It is now almost a suburb of Yarmouth. Blessed with a long sandy beach, Gorleston has retained a distinct character of its own.

▼ **Gorleston, The Gardens and Bandstand 1908** 60659

The awnings are still up on the bandstand and the musicians are tuning up in readiness for the afternoon matinee. A colourful throng is being entertained by pierrots on the beach. The women are dressed for the warm weather, but the men swelter in their workaday suits and hats - the Edwardians had no special holiday outfits as we do today. Gorleston's pavilion was built in 1898.

▼ **Gorleston, The Sands 1894** 33392

A young man enjoys the broad prospect of Gorleston sands from the worn and pocked cliff. The ports of East Anglia have suffered continual erosion down the centuries. The mouths of the Rivers Bure, Yare and Waveney were joined through silting above Yarmouth and now flow south to the sea at Gorleston.

▲ **Gorleston, The Harbour 1894** 33393
The fishing fleet, having waited patiently for a breeze, can at last set sail in pursuit of the herring. In the heyday of the industry the quays would have been thronged with fisher girls gutting the catch. Little more than a decade later most of the sailing barges had been replaced by steam-driven vessels.

◀ **Gorleston, High Street 1908** 60664
Not to be outdone by its more prestigious neighbour Yarmouth, Gorleston constructed its own tramway. On the right a pub has sprung up to capitalise on the new custom, calling itself 'The Tramway Hotel'. In the background is an open-top tram - what better way to enjoy the sea air?

Gorleston, High Street 1908 60663
A number twenty-eight tram slides silently along the High Street. The streets are deserted, so everyone must be down at the beach enjoying the sun and sea breezes. Gorleston had a reputation for healthy living - in the churchyard are eight gravestones celebrating centenarians.

Hopton, The Holiday Camp c1955 H310084
Hopton is a diminutive village resort on the A12 just south of Great Yarmouth. Here holiday makers could enjoy the quiet attractions of the 'Constitutional Holiday Camp' well away from the bustle and bright lights of its noisier and bigger neighbour. Every effort has been made to intensify the holiday atmosphere: there are 'cabin' style chalets daubed with bright colours, rustic seats, flower-bedded lawns and plenty of beach space.

Caister on Sea, High Street c1955 C450078
Although there are many pleasant cottages in the vernacular brick and flint, the modest village street does not reflect Caister's illustrious history. Caister's Castle was built by Sir John Fastolf when he returned from the French wars. Having led the English archers at Agincourt, he was seeking well-deserved repose and retirement. The castle later passed to the Paston family, its chequered history described in their famous letters.

Caister on Sea c1955 C450012
A few stalwart holidaymakers are enjoying the giddy sport of roller-skating on the holiday camp rink. Some go gingerly round in pairs in an effort to keep their feet. It looks like it is a cold day, for the spectators are wearing their overcoats.

Caister on Sea, The Holiday Camp c1955
C450025
For many working people life after the War was gray and utilitarian. Holiday camps like Caister's offered inexpensive breaks for the whole family - with all costs included. The chalets were spartan, but there was the certainty of meeting new friends as well as a plethora of free activities. A good time was assured for all. The family tricycle was always a popular attraction.

Caister on Sea, The Sands c1955 C450081
Each holiday camp had its own stretch of beach for the exclusive use of guests. Here children are enjoying donkey rides on a breezy summer's day. Special holiday outfits have still not been introduced, for the boys are wearing their school blazers.

Once a strategic Roman station, this coastal village is now almost a suburb of Great Yarmouth. The town is renowned for the bravery of its lifeboat crew who responded to an urgent signal of distress in 1901. Nine crew were lost and a tribute to their courage and selflessness is to be found in the churchyard: 'Caister men never turn back, sir'.

The Broads

The Broads have been a watery playground for holidaymakers for decades. It is hard to believe that these broad expanses of smooth water are man-made. In medieval times peat was dug on a grand scale and the landscape would have appeared very different. The diggings were originally dry, resembling great open-cast mines, and were prone to flooding and inundation during periods of rising water levels.

The Broads, Mill and River c1934 T213064
This placid scene depicts the Broads as every water traveller would wish to experience them. There is no jostling, no locks nor congested passages, simply a broad silent water fringed with reed beds and an historic windmill.

◄ **The Broads, The Navigable Limit c1955**

T213066

Much of the surrounding countryside is at or below sea level. Here a cottage squats just a few feet above the level of the waters. It is not surprising that inhabitants were regularly displaced from their homes. A massive control scheme of dykes and sluices was engineered in the 17th century.

The Broads, The Evening Ferry c1900
T213073
Sunset against sombre skies, dark shadowy trees, an invisible breeze, the slap of waters among the reeds... a woman in pinafore dress and bonnet punts her way home after the day's toil. This atmospheric scene captures the essential spirit of the Broads with their solitary backwaters.

▼ Acle, The Folly Tree c1950 A204081
The busy trunk road to Norwich winds through the heart of Acle past many pleasing old houses. Years before, in 1869, a Mr Thorn stopped to catch his breath here during a pioneering ride to Norwich on his new-fangled bicycle velocipede, 'so much in vogue in Paris'. His progress was 'considerably retarded by the roughness of the roads and a powerful gale'. The town boasts a thriving and established market for store pigs.

◄ Acle, Fishing at the Bridge c1929 A204037
As one old guide book pointed out, 'To every broadsman who quants his wherry along the slow rivers, Acle Bridge is a haven or port of call. Many are the little ships of adventure which lower their masts and sails to pass beneath'. The early Victorian bridge was once the scene of more dubious activities - criminals were executed here by being hung from the parapet.

Acle c1929 A204048
Though the Broads are
wild and empty places
of sweeping skies and
wind-blown marshes,
the traveller by boat is
never far from history.
The marshland all
around, much of it
reclaimed from the sea,
is dissected by dykes,
the grazing parcelled
out by ancient custom.
Here a 17th-century
windmill wheezily turns
its battered sails. At
Acle there is a
minuscule priory
founded by Roger
Bigod.

Acle, The Entrance to the River Thurne c1926 A204049
The Thurne is a tributary of the Bure, winding through vast, flat landscapes of salt marsh. Many of the buildings here are perilously below sea level. Some of the old windmills that grace its banks have been lovingly restored but, of course, no longer carry out their original task of draining the marshes.

Reedham, The Ferry c1955 R303072
Reedham, in the broad, silent expanses of the Yare valley, was once a thriving North sea port. The chain ferry pictured offers the only passage across the Yare between Norwich and Yarmouth. Windmills are dotted among the abundant reedbeds, from which the village gained its name.

Cantley, The Red House Hotel c1965 C414004
Set on the banks of the River Yare, Cantley is dominated by its sugar refinery, which was built to process local beet. Customers at The Red House could not only see its smoke but also watch a steady stream of vessels hauling freights up to Norwich. There is a fine church with a Norman doorway.

Horning 1934 86364
Horning is blessed with a wealth of reed-thatched cottages with eyebrowed dormers, as well as other more unusual buildings - the house alongside where the car is parked has crow-stepped gables, revealing a Dutch influence. Horning is fortunate to have retained much of its Edwardian charm, unlike some of its brasher, more commercial neighbours.

Horning 1934 86365
This charming village
straddles the banks of
the River Bure amidst
beautiful marshland. Set
in the heart of
Broadland, it has been
called 'little Venice',
with soft green lawns
spreading down to the
water's edge. In the
summer months it is
thronged with pleasure
boats, and all is bustle
and noise. Here village
policemen are directing
the summer traffic. The
Horning branch of Roy's
of Wroxham proclaims
itself 'the biggest
village store in the
world'. By the door
there is a carousel
display of local postcard
views by one of Francis
Frith's major rivals,
Raphael Tuck.

▼ **Horning 1902** 48110

Broadland is strewn with relics of previous ages. Here an old wind pump, its sails still set against the breeze, takes on the character of a living tree with its roughly-hewn timber supports. Such pumps were vital to assist drainage on wet lands and were in use until the middle of the 20th century.

▼ **Horning, St Benet's Abbey Ruins c1955** H116160

Amidst the Cowholm marshes are the scanty ruins of St Benet's Abbey, founded by Canute. It has the reputation of being the only abbey not dissolved at the Dissolution, its revenues continuing to provide an income for the Bishop of Norwich. Within its bounds a marshland drainage mill was built many years ago, its smooth, conical form combining curiously with the jagged broken masonry of the old gatehouse.

▲ **Horning, On the Broads 1902** 48108

When sailing wherry you had to be able to sail very close to the wind, for the narrow waterways allowed no extravagant tacking manoeuvres. It was unwise to touch bottom either, especially when the boat was low in the water and loaded with freight. Built of local oak, the gaff-rigged wherry was precisely designed for Broadland conditions, and fleets of them once plied between Yarmouth and Norwich.

◀ **Horning 1902** 48107
A young woman, elegantly
dressed in long skirt and
white blouse, tends her
cabbage patch. She has
drawn her row boat up on
the sand alongside the ivy-
encrusted boathouse. All
around is a scene of utter
rural peace.

Hoveton 1921 70890
At Hoveton there is a
full mile of shimmering
open water which is
thronged with pleasure
craft in the summer
months. The capital of
the Broads is Wroxham
which is just across the
bridge. It is a popular
starting point for boating
holidays which grew
rapidly in the early years
of this century. An old
street trader has pushed
his hand cart into the
middle of the street and
nonchalantly weighs out
vegetables regardless of
passing traffic. He must
make the most of his
monopoly: a competitor,
his cart overladen with
trays of fresh fruit and
vegetables, is hurrying
towards the junction.

Hoveton c1950 H399112

Three decades later, the quiet cross ways of the previous view present a very different character. Roy's, 'the biggest village shop in the world' has plumped itself over two corners. The proprietors are after the visitors' holiday money: there are signs for chocolate, cards, Kodak film, millinery, soft drinks, toilet requisites... and in the distance hoardings advertise trips on the Broads, Judges postcards, guides and maps, Goss china and newspapers.

Hoveton c1950 H399113

Here Roy's have blatantly disregarded any concern for harmonising vernacular. This brash and kitsch 1920s art deco building clearly intends to convey the impression of a temple of delights. Visitors are encouraged to buy Wroxham rock and are invited to 'walk through this store without being pressed to buy'.

Wroxham, On the Bure 1921 70893
A mile from Wroxham Broad and spanning the Bure is this lovely old single-span bridge, partially hidden by a passing sail. Gardens slope down to the river, and thick canopies of trees at the water's edge keep the wind from the sails of boats. The banks of the Bure here are pitted with artificial basins, where boats lie up in safety during the long months of winter.

Wroxham Broad 1934 86359
Wroxham Broad winds through solitary, yet fertile countryside. It is almost impossible to believe that this huge stretch of placid water was hacked out by men seeking fuel for their hearths. A woman sits on the shards of a rotted hulk gazing out at the heeling yachts.

◀ **Belaugh, The Church from the River 1921**

70898

St Peter's Church perches on a lofty crest overlooking the River Bure which twists through a series of loops below. Following in the Norfolk tradition of fine churches, St Peter's is a noble if diminutive edifice, with a fine old traceried screen and Norman font.

◄ **Coltishall, A Cornfield 1902** 48127
This classic farming scene depicts an age now sadly gone. Sheaves of wheat are heaped in wind-blown stooks. A white-bearded old farmer, resplendent in smock and battered hat, poses with his granddaughter. Today so much of East Anglia's beautiful countryside is in the hands of more exploitative 'barley barons'.

▼ **Coltishall 1902** 48166
Horses graze the rich meadows that keep the waters of the Bure from the village street. Here are handsome pantile-roofed red-brick houses. A rotted hulk squats in a narrow inlet. To the left are shallow-roofed warehouses.

◄ **Horstead Mill, near Coltishall 1902** 48150
The decking of the square-rigged wherry 'Widgeon' has been lifted away in sections for its cargo of planks to be offloaded - they are stacked neatly under the stone arches of the mill. In the foreground a small boy is fishing.

Horstead Mill, near Coltishall 1902 48149
The 'Widgeon' is drawn up alongside the mill offloading its cargo. Fully laden, such wherries would only draw a little over two feet, making them the perfect vessels for navigating the shallow waters of the Broads. Note the single high-peaked mainsail, the considerable height allowing the craft to collect every last puff of wind that passed over the thick canopy of trees fringing the banks.

Coltishall, The River 1902 48159

An old boatman with a bright neckerchief sits on his oars, having rowed a passenger to this quiet backwater amongst the reedbeds. She stands at the water's edge enjoying the birdsong and the vistas of open water. It is late afternoon and at last there are long, cool shadows to refresh the weary.

North Walsham, Market Place 1921 70936

Much of this prosperous market town, north of the Broads, was rebuilt after a major fire in 1600. Its pleasing Georgian facades spread round the market place. North Walsham was once a significant weaving centre. Its prosperity was increased after a canal was dug connecting the River Ant with the Broads.

Old Windpump, Near Ludham c1955 L110082
Ludham sits on 'high' ground, which in Broadland can be just a few feet above sea level. The flat lands around are threaded by three great rivers, the Thurne, Ant and Bure. The old windpump at Turf Fen, its sails now still, offers testament to man's battle with the rising waters down the centuries.

Potter Heigham, The Bridge 1934 86381
The old medieval stone bridge, with one central and two pointed side arches, carries Yarmouth-bound traffic over the Thurne. Its painted warning 'Caution, proceed slowly' must not be ignored. Generations ago, even the great trading wherries had to halt and drop their masts to gain passage. Today the village is mainly the province of pleasure craft, who clog the quays in the months of summer.

Potter Heigham c1926 P167007
The bridge has endured the excesses of the Broadland waters for many centuries, yet it required continual repairs and bolstering up - buttresses have been added to keep it in service. The old wooden hut on the bank is sliding inevitably down into the shallows, its thatched roof rotted and patched.

Hickling, The Pleasure Boat Inn c1955 H307011
At Hickling, where the Broadland waters fan into expansive shallows, there is a pleasing jumble of red tiled and thatched buildings clustering around the old Pleasure Boat Inn. John of Oxnead, a monk at nearby St Benet's Abbey, recounts how, in 1287, the sea burst in upon the flat shorelands and the town of 'Hyckelnygge'.

Horsey, The Mere c1955 H341009
This tiny settlement is set in a remote area of the Broads, where willows and reed beds thrust out into the waters narrowing the passage. It looks peaceful enough, but it is just two miles from the coast, and down by the dunes the sea blows unrelentingly. On many unforgettable nights at high tide, angry seas have broken through the banks and flooded many thousands of acres of farmland.

Cromer and the North Coast

Set high above the sea, but sheltered by wooded hills, Cromer was once was little more than a jumble of simple cottages huddled around the church, and the exclusive haunt of fishermen and crabbers. The town burgeoned into a popular resort with the coming of the railways. Only Yarmouth attracts more visitors.

Cromer, The Sands 1899 44482
Building work carried on apace in the town in an attempt to keep up with the influx of visitors. Hotels and lodging houses sprang up in the narrow streets radiating out from the church square. On the right are bathing machines which have been towed down into the water so that ladies could enjoy discreet dips in the shallows.

Cromer, From the West 1906 56850
It can be a long dangerous slide down the tiered sea walls to the sands and pier. The smart new flight of steps allowed ladies in long dresses to make a dignified descent. One Edwardian visitor recalls an excursion to Cromer in a wagon lent by a local farmer. He sent a postcard to his mother to let her know he had arrived safely. It was delivered by the afternoon post the same day!

◀ **Cromer, The Pier 1902**
49062
Cromer's 500ft-long pier was built in 1901 to replace a landing jetty destroyed by gales in 1897. In the storms of 1953 it was damaged again. A young woman stands with her grandmother a little along from the Bath Hotel. They encapsulate the fundamental changes in fashion that occurred during the first years of our century - the grandmother must be sweltering in her dark, burdensome Victorian gown.

◀ Cromer, From the Sea 1902
49059

The 160ft tower of the mainly Perpendicular church of St Peter and St Paul soars majestically over the town and is a prominent day mark for shipping in the choppy coastal waters. The tower once acted as a lighthouse and is the second loftiest in Norfolk after that of Norwich Cathedral.

▼ Cromer, The Promenade 1902 49069

Architects, like everyone else, tend to fling off their inhibitions at the seaside. Here a Chinese-inspired pagoda with veranda provides a welcome spot for visitors to repose out of the sun. A gentle stroll up the promenade before lunch was *de rigeur* for the Edwardian holidaymaker.

◀ Cromer, The Sands 1899 44485

The beach was the centre of fun and frivolity. The flags are flying and a throng of holidaymakers waits to board a fleet of row boats for a trip along the coast. Though Cromer crabs were famous and plentiful, the Cromer fishermen welcomed the opportunity to make a few extra shillings from the summer trade with their boats.

Cromer, The Lifeboat 1922 72651
Cromer's lifeboatmen are renowned for their gallantry. Henry Blogg, coxswain of the 'Louisa Heartwell', pictured here, was the most decorated lifeboatman in Britain, earning three gold and four silver medals, the George Cross and the British Empire medal for his bravery. Most of the Cromer rescues were carried out on the treacherous Haisboro' Sands.

Cromer, The Lighthouse 1894 33325
A young lad sits on the grass on the sheltered inward side of the cliffs. The new lighthouse perches on the most prominent point, its powerful beam sweeping nightly across the dark sky and spilling its light over the walls of the parish church like a searchlight. The church itself was once used as a sea mark by mariners.

Cromer, Garden Street 1894 33330
A view towards the sea along a quiet backstreet of Edwardian terraces. Many of these houses rented out rooms to summer lodgers who were unable to afford bed and board in more prestigious hotels. Mortimer's shop on the right is offering rolls of decorative linoleum and dress fabrics.

East Runton, High Street 1921 70970
East Runton offered visitors the same spectacular cliff scenery and ample beaches as its close neighbour, Cromer, but less of the noise and bustle. The Edwardian terraces in the foreground, with their bay windows and neat gardens and railings, harmonise with the simpler cottages beyond.

East Runton, The Beach Entrance 1921 70968
At East Runton you could walk out along broad stretches of beach and enjoy digging for fossils in the soft cliffs, a pastime made popular by the Victorians. If you wished to swim you had to exercise extreme caution - bathing could be a perilous affair because of strong currents and swift tides.

▼ **East Runton, Looking East 1933** 85828
Poorly compacted, and composed of glacial drift, the cliffs of the
north Norfolk coast have been compared to 'dirty tallow', being
unstable and liable to erosion. A row of white beach huts trims the
foot of the cliffs like a cuff. In the distance is Cromer pier.

▼ **Sheringham, High Street 1901** 46544
The town comprises two villages, Upper and Lower Sheringham, the former more
peaceful and retaining its fishing and farming traditions. Some of the High Street
shops and houses reveal a Dutch influence, with mansard roofs and ornamental
gables. The blinds are down, it is a hot day. Developments away from exclusive
local suppliers in retailing are already apparent, with Lincoln's offering 'choicest
New Zealand mutton, fresh every morning'.

▲ **Sheringham 1893**
33311
A typically ramshackle
fishermen's scene, with
boats drawn up on the
shingle, which is littered
with maritime
paraphernalia. As tourism
expanded, and smart
visitors arrived in ever
greater numbers, such
untidiness was frowned
on by local businesses -
the town had to smarten
up its image.

◄ **Sheringham, The Church 1894** 33316
Noble trees cluster round the churchyard wall. The public drinking fountain, decorated with embedded pebbles, was constructed in the 1820s. The lane is plain compacted mud. In winter it would be treacherous. To the south of the town is remote heath and woodland.

Sheringham, Fishermen 1893

33313

The railway reached the fishing hamlet of Sheringham ten years later than its close neighbour, Cromer. Even then the trains arrived only from the Midlands and the North. It was not until 1906 that the line from Cromer was extended to the town. Less disturbed by the outside world, the close-linked fishing community endured a little longer, and the inevitable development was more restrained. Sheringham fishermen pursued not only crabs and lobsters but herring, cod and whiting. They were the traditional enemies of Cromer men, who referred to them disparagingly as 'Shaddocks'. Nets were regularly cut and battles fought. However, with their hats set at a rakish angle, these Sheringham fishermen look formidable adversaries.

Sheringham, Fishermen 1906 56880
Fishing was a rough and dangerous way to earn a living. The North Sea tides could prove fatal for small craft, and more than once the Cromer lifeboat was forced out into bad weather to rescue whelkers. These men are suitably dressed for foul conditions in their thigh-length sea boots and thick fishermen's ganseys.

Sheringham, The Beach 1901 46540
Sheringham fishermen gather round a lobster boat for the camera. They ventured out in open boats in all weathers. Proud and independent, they looked to each other in danger and adversity, sharing not just their perilous profession but their religion - most were devout Salvationists.

Cley-next-the-Sea 1933 85836
This picturesque flint village was once the most significant of the Glaven estuary ports, and its old Custom House bears testimony to its prestigious past. Silting of the waterway presaged the decline of Cley's influence, and coastal vessels now pass it by. The fine old windmill dates from 1713, and guards the town from the open marshlands.

Blakeney, The Regatta c1955 B121087
Standing on the fringes of the Norfolk marshes, Blakeney like Cley, once knew busier days. Its capacious natural harbour, protected from the sea by the long spit of sand, Blakeney Point, attracted coastal trading vessels until the early years of this century. The landscape offers birdwatchers an irresistible mixture of dunes, saltings, mud-flats and creeks.

▼ **Blakeney c1955** B121025

The town is studded with fine brick and flint houses with steep pantiled roofs - on the right is the flamboyant brick and pebble Barclay's Bank. Hayward's the confectioner and newsagent, on the left, has retained its attractive wooden facia and ornamental painted signboard.

▼ **Wells-next-the-Sea 1929** 81996

From Wells to Blakeney, a great sand barrier holds back all but the most vicious tides. The quay at Wells is now stranded a mile from the open sea. The harbour was developed by the railway companies - wagons of the London Midland Scottish Line are drawn up at the quayside. In the background is a medley of vintage buildings, some with crow-stepped gables characteristic of the Low Countries, reflecting the town's historic trading links.

▲ **Wells-next-the-Sea, The Quay 1929** 81998

The Wells whelkers are renowned along this coast for their persistence in pursuing their trade. Whelking was not always a comfortable affair. Dropping pots from open clinker-built boats in pitch darkness and foul weather meant the whelkers could often find themselves stranded for hours on end on the wrong side of the bar waiting for the tide.

◀ **Wells-next-the-Sea, Bringing in the Cockles 1929** 82003
The limitless flat salt marshes stretch out beyond the narrow channel. These heavily-laden fishermen use shoulder yokes to carry their shellfish, much as a milkmaid carries her buckets, paddling out of the shallows from their open boats, the 'Nell' and 'Armistice'. A few modest coastal vessels still unload here but Blakeney has now given itself over to summer tourism.

Wells-next-the-Sea c1955 W48061
The cottages in this alley still retain a simple charm. The house on the left has been given rough repairs for generations - its toppling dormer lacks several panes of glass. Wells has suffered more than most Norfolk towns from the impact of incomers. In the years since this picture was taken many of its old buildings have either been demolished or tidied up beyond recognition.

Barningham Hall 1922 72671

This sumptuous red-brick Hall, set in exquisite parkland, was built by Sir William Paston in the early 1600s, and its facade is a grand example of Jacobean work. Repton remodelled it in 1805 and added the bow-windows. The church is still in service and stands in the park, although the nave and tower have been ruinous since the 1600s.

Aldborough c1955 A278013

Set a short distance away from the Cromer to Norwich road, Aldborough offers a spacious prospect with cottages grouped round a broad green. East Anglian villages, built on cleared common land, so often enjoy a handsome central space, echoing the broad skies overhead. The village has a watermill alongside the River Bure.

▼ **Aldborough c1955** A278003

Fisher's store is selling Raleigh, Rudge and Humber cycles. To its right is a fish and chip shop, which surely must rely on a good degree of passing trade. The 'Black Boys', with its multi-paned windows and pantiled roof, is a classic village inn, small and intimate.

▼ **Holt, Market Place 1896** 37977

The shop on the extreme right has an imposing display of bamboo baskets, chairs and hatstands, and a wide variety of galvanised tinware. It also reveals a somewhat insensitive example of infill, no attempt having been made by the architect to follow the existing roof line.

Holt, High Street 1896
37976
Holt, between Fakenham and Cromer, boasts a wealth of fine Georgian houses, which huddle haphazardly around its broad market place. It was rebuilt all of a piece after a devastating fire in 1708. On the left is a fine Victorian shopfront imposed on a plain brick house. The town is renowned for its public school, Gresham's, founded in 1555 by John Gresham, Lord Mayor of London.

▶ Walsingham, Priory Gateway 1922 72628
Founded in 1149, the priory was renowned throughout Europe. All that is left today is a tantalising ruin in the grounds of Walsingham Abbey, with fragments of wall and window and two old wishing wells. No traces remain of the holy shrine, though it is still a place of pilgrimage for devout Catholics.

Walsingham, Sheep Going to Market 1929

82040

Walsingham is built around the ruins of a monastic house, celebrated for its shrine to Our Lady of Walsingham. It is an important place of pilgrimage, second only to Becket's tomb at Canterbury. Fringed by rich woodland, and with a medieval well, priory and many splendid timber-framed houses, Walsingham retains a powerful historic and religious atmosphere for visitors.

This old shepherd, plodding on to Walsingham market, has been enjoying a glass of ale in the 'White Hart'. His sheep have just been sheared, and are watched over by his dog in the foreground. Shepherds lived lonely lives, and the occasional journeys into market were welcome occasions to hear the gossip and to discuss the farming year.

Hunstanton, High Street 1907 58898
Hunstanton is unique for north Norfolk resort towns in that it looks west across the sea and not east. It was a quiet village of simple fishermen's cottages until the coming of the railway in 1862. Then building began in earnest as visitors flocked to enjoy its safe, sandy beach and bracing cliff-top walks. In this High Street view there is a dairy, Preston's Library (where you could borrow a novel to enjoy whilst lounging in your deckchair), and a branch of International Stores, which quickly saw off old-style local competition.

Hunstanton, The Bathing Beach 1921 71030
Hunstanton had been described in the 1860s as 'a compact little watering place with everything on a miniature scale - a little railway station, six or seven bathing machines etc..' Sixty years later, in 1921, the bathing machines are still in evidence. The coast was particularly attractive with its striped chalk and carrstone cliffs, which rise to 60 feet. They are the seaward end of a ridge extending across the whole county.

Hunstanton, The Green 1901 47641
The new town is gathered around an expansive green. Hunstanton grew out of the hamlet of Hunstanton St Edmund, sited low on the cliffs and owned by the Le Strange family of the Hall. They saw its potential as a popular resort, and soon prestigious hotels were clothing the edges of the green.

Hunstanton, The Green 1907 58895
Genteel and intimate, Hunstanton attracted the more discerning visitor. Middle class children enjoy games of cricket. Their parents relax over newspapers and novels in the lounges of comfortable hotels. The Great Eastern Railway Company Hotel, shown in the background, was particularly popular.

▼ Hunstanton, The Pier c1955 H135072

With the town so resolutely proper, the pier was the mecca for the feckless pleasure-seeker. Noisy and colourful, it offered a myriad pleasures. The signboard proclaims: 'For Your Entertainment, Bingo, Rock Stall, Wax Work Exhibition, Soda Fountain, Acrobatics, Bazaar and Skating'. The pier has since been demolished, having been damaged by gales in the 1970s.

▼ Heacham, High Street c1955 H57084

This small village sits between the sea and fields of bright lavender. At Caley Mill there is a lavender water distillery, and in late summer the fields shimmer with a deep blue. The railway from Heacham to Wells was a lifeline for the export of local grain, vegetables, bricks and shellfish for metropolitan markets.

▲ Hunstanton, The Lighthouse 1891 28773

Hunstanton's lighthouse was built in 1830, and crowns the chalk clifftop close by the ruins of St Edmund's chapel, where pilgrims offered their prayers and sought the healing powers of the town's efficacious springs. Legend has it that Edmund, before becoming king of East Anglia, was almost shipwrecked here in treacherous seas, and founded the chapel in gratitude to God for sparing his life.

**◄ Sandringham House
1896** 38391
This exquisite royal estate was purchased by Queen Victoria for her beloved Prince of Wales in 1861. Within its 7,000 acres are the lands of seven parishes, and a profusion of deep woods, sandy heathland and broad grassy rides, which are the haunt of deer. The house was built a decade later in the Tudor style, a cumbersome confection of stone and red brick.

King's Lynn and Around

This illustrious and sublime town is on the east bank of the River Ouse, two miles from the Wash. Silting of the Ouse's ponderous waters robbed the town of much of its former prestige as a seaport, but its many graceful buildings and old Custom House have brought to it the appellation of 'most romantic town in England'.

Left: **King's Lynn, Southgate 1891** 28760
Friars Fleet winds along the back of the town and joins the Ouse close by the quay. King's Lynn flourished into one of richest ports in the land in medieval times. Cargoes of wool, cloth from Flanders, and timber from the Baltic crossed into England here. In the 19th century the quays were still busy, but with coastal craft carrying corn, hauled up the fenland rivers, to be transported on to London. Southgate is a remnant of the old town walls.

Below: **King's Lynn, The South Gate 1925** 78716
The East Gate to the town was demolished in 1800, but the old South Gate on the road from London still stands. Built in the 15th century, it has imposing battlements and turrets, and is of brick faced with stone.

King's Lynn, High Street 1908 60024
This street of small distinctive shops and handsome 18th-century terraced buildings is the commercial hub of the town. Spanning the street are a pair of open decorative iron arches on which are hung the town lamps. On the left is a formidable display of boots and shoes cascading over the shop facia.

King's Lynn, The Tuesday Market 1898 40886
Lynn's market place is one of the very finest in England, enriched by a profusion of Georgian and Victorian public buildings, including the florid Corn Exchange built in 1854. This scene would have changed little over many hundreds of years: farmers' wives travelled in by pony and trap to sell their fresh fruit and vegetables, and market traders shouted for business from below colourful awnings.

King's Lynn, High Street 1908 60023
Jermyn and Perry's considerable premises dominate this busy High Street scene. Their display is spectacular, with hats, parasols, curtains and bolts of cloth tumbling out on to the pavement in a visual feast. It would surely have required a staff of full-time window-dressers to maintain. Outside, a young lad propels his baby sister around in an orange box on wheels. The business was later taken over by Debenham's.

King's Lynn, The Custom House 1898 40878
The Purfleet, with its low bridge, is an old tidal inlet of the Ouse. Here stands the exquisite Custom House of 1683, with its graceful classical-style facade. It began life as the Merchants' Exchange, with an open-arched arcade on the ground floor. This was blocked in 1718 when the building was converted for use as a Customs House.

◀ **North Wootton, The Post Office 1908** 60035
Mr and Mrs Raines ran an efficient postal service from this humble shed at the bottom of their garden for many years - there was surely hardly room to swing a mail sack. The slot through which villagers poked their letters is at the left hand corner. The village was, of course, much smaller then, with just four sizeable families and a dozen cottages.

King's Lynn, The Town Hall and Guildhall 1891 28754

This magnificent tour de force of flint and stone chequerwork was built in 1421 for the Guild of Holy Trinity, a wealthy group of merchants. Above the many-mullioned rectangular window of the porch are the arms of Edward the Sixth and Elizabeth. Many civic treasures are held within, including the Red Book of Lynn, in which are recorded the municipal records from 1204 to 1392. The matching town hall was built in 1895.

▼ Downham Market, The Castle Hotel c1950 D149020

The Castle Hotel looks iced as exuberantly as a birthday cake. The extravagant frontage, with its battlements, Venetian window and heavy rustication, was added to a simpler, more homely facade in the 18th century. Such facings were popular, for they created a fresh, fashionable character, without the necessity for wholesale demolition and rebuilding.

◀ Downham Market, High Street c1950

D149011

Banks have always been notorious for over-embellishing their premises in small market towns. Here, Lloyds Bank has created a classical porch that must have intimidated customers seeking loans. Often banks demolished fine old Georgian buildings and replaced them with premises that completely disregarded the prevailing local style.

Downham Market, The Clock Tower c1950 D149010

Like so many of its neighbours, Downham Market was a river port of some importance until railway workings cut it off from the waters of the Ouse. Perched on high ground at the fringes of the Fens, it is a place that conceals its long history - rich finds of Romano-British pottery confirm that it was a considerable settlement in Roman times, with peat being dug in huge quantities. The town presents a mellow and harmonious face to the visitor. The buildings ranged around the market place are of yellow and brown brick and Norfolk carr stone. The clock, in florid Gothic style, was erected in 1878 by William Cunliffe.

Index

Frith Book Co Titles

www.francisfrith.co.uk

The Frith Book Company publishes over 100 new titles each year. A selection of those currently available are listed below. For latest catalogue please contact Frith Book Co.

Town Books 96 pages, approx 100 photos. County and Themed Books 128 pages, approx 150 photos (unless specified). All titles hardback laminated case and jacket except those indicated pb (paperback)

Amersham, Chesham & Rickmansworth (pb)			Derby (pb)	1-85937-367-4	£9.99
	1-85937-340-2	£9.99	Derbyshire (pb)	1-85937-196-5	£9.99
Ancient Monuments & Stone Circles	1-85937-143-4	£17.99	Devon (pb)	1-85937-297-x	£9.99
Aylesbury (pb)	1-85937-227-9	£9.99	Dorset (pb)	1-85937-269-4	£9.99
Bakewell	1-85937-113-2	£12.99	Dorset Churches	1-85937-172-8	£17.99
Barnstaple (pb)	1-85937-300-3	£9.99	Dorset Coast (pb)	1-85937-299-6	£9.99
Bath (pb)	1-85937419-0	£9.99	Dorset Living Memories	1-85937-210-4	£14.99
Bedford (pb)	1-85937-205-8	£9.99	Down the Severn	1-85937-118-3	£14.99
Berkshire (pb)	1-85937-191-4	£9.99	Down the Thames (pb)	1-85937-278-3	£9.99
Berkshire Churches	1-85937-170-1	£17.99	Down the Trent	1-85937-311-9	£14.99
Blackpool (pb)	1-85937-382-8	£9.99	Dublin (pb)	1-85937-231-7	£9.99
Bognor Regis (pb)	1-85937-431-x	£9.99	East Anglia (pb)	1-85937-265-1	£9.99
Bournemouth	1-85937-067-5	£12.99	East London	1-85937-080-2	£14.99
Bradford (pb)	1-85937-204-x	£9.99	East Sussex	1-85937-130-2	£14.99
Brighton & Hove(pb)	1-85937-192-2	£8.99	Eastbourne	1-85937-061-6	£12.99
Bristol (pb)	1-85937-264-3	£9.99	Edinburgh (pb)	1-85937-193-0	£8.99
British Life A Century Ago (pb)	1-85937-213-9	£9.99	England in the 1880s	1-85937-331-3	£17.99
Buckinghamshire (pb)	1-85937-200-7	£9.99	English Castles (pb)	1-85937-434-4	£9.99
Camberley (pb)	1-85937-222-8	£9.99	English Country Houses	1-85937-161-2	£17.99
Cambridge (pb)	1-85937-422-0	£9.99	Essex (pb)	1-85937-270-8	£9.99
Cambridgeshire (pb)	1 85937 420 4	£9.99	Exeter	1-85937-126-4	£12.99
Canals & Waterways (pb)	1-85937-291-0	£9.99	Exmoor	1-85937-132-9	£14.99
Canterbury Cathedral (pb)	1-85937-179-5	£9.99	Falmouth	1-85937-066-7	£12.99
Cardiff (pb)	1-85937-093-4	£9.99	Folkestone (pb)	1-85937-124-8	£9.99
Carmarthenshire	1-85937-216-3	£14.99	Glasgow (pb)	1-85937-190-6	£9.99
Chelmsford (pb)	1-85937-310-0	£9.99	Gloucestershire	1-85937-102-7	£14.99
Cheltenham (pb)	1-85937-095-0	£9.99	Great Yarmouth (pb)	1-85937-426-3	£9.99
Cheshire (pb)	1-85937-271-6	£9.99	Greater Manchester (pb)	1-85937-266-x	£9.99
Chester	1-85937-090-x	£12.99	Guildford (pb)	1-85937-410-7	£9.99
Chesterfield	1-85937-378-x	£9.99	Hampshire (pb)	1-85937-279-1	£9.99
Chichester (pb)	1-85937-228-7	£9.99	Hampshire Churches (pb)	1-85937-207-4	£9.99
Colchester (pb)	1-85937-188-4	£8.99	Harrogate	1-85937-423-9	£9.99
Cornish Coast	1-85937-163-9	£14.99	Hastings & Bexhill (pb)	1-85937-131-0	£9.99
Cornwall (pb)	1-85937-229-5	£9.99	Heart of Lancashire (pb)	1-85937-197-3	£9.99
Cornwall Living Memories	1-85937-248-1	£14.99	Helston (pb)	1-85937-214-7	£9.99
Cotswolds (pb)	1-85937-230-9	£9.99	Hereford (pb)	1-85937-175-2	£9.99
Cotswolds Living Memories	1-85937-255-4	£14.99	Herefordshire	1-85937-174-4	£14.99
County Durham	1-85937-123-x	£14.99	Hertfordshire (pb)	1-85937-247-3	£9.99
Croydon Living Memories	1-85937-162-0	£9.99	Horsham (pb)	1-85937-432-8	£9.99
Cumbria	1-85937-101-9	£14.99	Humberside	1-85937-215-5	£14.99
Dartmoor	1-85937-145-0	£14.99	Hythe, Romney Marsh & Ashford	1-85937-256-2	£9.99

Available from your local bookshop or from the publisher

Frith Book Co Titles (continued)

Ipswich (pb)	1-85937-424-7	£9.99	St Ives (pb)	1-85937415-8	£9.99
Ireland (pb)	1-85937-181-7	£9.99	Scotland (pb)	1-85937-182-5	£9.99
Isle of Man (pb)	1-85937-268-6	£9.99	Scottish Castles (pb)	1-85937-323-2	£9.99
Isles of Scilly	1-85937-136-1	£14.99	Sevenoaks & Tunbridge	1-85937-057-8	£12.99
Isle of Wight (pb)	1-85937-429-8	£9.99	Sheffield, South Yorks (pb)	1-85937-267-8	£9.99
Isle of Wight Living Memories	1-85937-304-6	£14.99	Shrewsbury (pb)	1-85937-325-9	£9.99
Kent (pb)	1-85937-189-2	£9.99	Shropshire (pb)	1-85937-326-7	£9.99
Kent Living Memories	1-85937-125-6	£14.99	Somerset	1-85937-153-1	£14.99
Lake District (pb)	1-85937-275-9	£9.99	South Devon Coast	1-85937-107-8	£14.99
Lancaster, Morecambe & Heysham (pb)	1-85937-233-3	£9.99	South Devon Living Memories	1-85937-168-x	£14.99
Leeds (pb)	1-85937-202-3	£9.99	South Hams	1-85937-220-1	£14.99
Leicester	1-85937-073-x	£12.99	Southampton (pb)	1-85937-427-1	£9.99
Leicestershire (pb)	1-85937-185-x	£9.99	Southport (pb)	1-85937-425-5	£9.99
Lincolnshire (pb)	1-85937-433-6	£9.99	Staffordshire	1-85937-047-0	£12.99
Liverpool & Merseyside (pb)	1-85937-234-1	£9.99	Stratford upon Avon	1-85937-098-5	£12.99
London (pb)	1-85937-183-3	£9.99	Suffolk (pb)	1-85937-221-x	£9.99
Ludlow (pb)	1-85937-176-0	£9.99	Suffolk Coast	1-85937-259-7	£14.99
Luton (pb)	1-85937-235-x	£9.99	Surrey (pb)	1-85937-240-6	£9.99
Maidstone	1-85937-056-x	£14.99	Sussex (pb)	1-85937-184-1	£9.99
Manchester (pb)	1-85937-198-1	£9.99	Swansea (pb)	1-85937-167-1	£9.99
Middlesex	1-85937-158-2	£14.99	Tees Valley & Cleveland	1-85937-211-2	£14.99
New Forest	1-85937-128-0	£14.99	Thanet (pb)	1-85937-116-7	£9.99
Newark (pb)	1-85937-366-6	£9.99	Tiverton (pb)	1-85937-178-7	£9.99
Newport, Wales (pb)	1-85937-258-9	£9.99	Torbay	1-85937-063-2	£12.99
Newquay (pb)	1-85937-421-2	£9.99	Truro	1-85937-147-7	£12.99
Norfolk (pb)	1-85937-195-7	£9.99	Victorian and Edwardian Cornwall	1-85937-252-x	£14.99
Norfolk Living Memories	1-85937-217-1	£14.99	Victorian & Edwardian Devon	1-85937-253-8	£14.99
Northamptonshire	1-85937-150-7	£14.99	Victorian & Edwardian Kent	1-85937-149-3	£14.99
Northumberland Tyne & Wear (pb)	1-85937-281-3	£9.99	Vic & Ed Maritime Album	1-85937-144-2	£17.99
North Devon Coast	1-85937-146-9	£14.99	Victorian and Edwardian Sussex	1-85937-157-4	£14.99
North Devon Living Memories	1-85937-261-9	£14.99	Victorian & Edwardian Yorkshire	1-85937-154-x	£14.99
North London	1-85937-206-6	£14.99	Victorian Seaside	1-85937-159-0	£17.99
North Wales (pb)	1-85937-298-8	£9.99	Villages of Devon (pb)	1-85937-293-7	£9.99
North Yorkshire (pb)	1-85937-236-8	£9.99	Villages of Kent (pb)	1-85937-294-5	£9.99
Norwich (pb)	1-85937-194-9	£8.99	Villages of Sussex (pb)	1-85937-295-3	£9.99
Nottingham (pb)	1-85937-324-0	£9.99	Warwickshire (pb)	1-85937-203-1	£9.99
Nottinghamshire (pb)	1-85937-187-6	£9.99	Welsh Castles (pb)	1-85937-322-4	£9.99
Oxford (pb)	1-85937-411-5	£9.99	West Midlands (pb)	1-85937-289-9	£9.99
Oxfordshire (pb)	1-85937-430-1	£9.99	West Sussex	1-85937-148-5	£14.99
Peak District (pb)	1-85937-280-5	£9.99	West Yorkshire (pb)	1-85937-201-5	£9.99
Penzance	1-85937-069-1	£12.99	Weymouth (pb)	1-85937-209-0	£9.99
Peterborough (pb)	1-85937-219-8	£9.99	Wiltshire (pb)	1-85937-277-5	£9.99
Piers	1-85937-237-6	£17.99	Wiltshire Churches (pb)	1-85937-171-x	£9.99
Plymouth	1-85937-119-1	£12.99	Wiltshire Living Memories	1-85937-245-7	£14.99
Poole & Sandbanks (pb)	1-85937-251-1	£9.99	Winchester (pb)	1-85937-428-x	£9.99
Preston (pb)	1-85937-212-0	£9.99	Windmills & Watermills	1-85937-242-2	£17.99
Reading (pb)	1-85937-238-4	£9.99	Worcester (pb)	1-85937-165-5	£9.99
Romford (pb)	1-85937-319-4	£9.99	Worcestershire	1-85937-152-3	£14.99
Salisbury (pb)	1-85937-239-2	£9.99	York (pb)	1-85937-199-x	£9.99
Scarborough (pb)	1-85937-379-8	£9.99	Yorkshire (pb)	1-85937-186-8	£9.99
St Albans (pb)	1-85937-341-0	£9.99	Yorkshire Living Memories	1-85937-166-3	£14.99

See Frith books on the internet www.francisfrith.co.uk

FRITH PRODUCTS & SERVICES

Francis Frith would doubtless be pleased to know that the pioneering publishing venture he started in 1860 still continues today. A hundred and forty years later, The Francis Frith Collection continues in the same innovative tradition and is now one of the foremost publishers of vintage photographs in the world. Some of the current activities include:

Interior Decoration

Today Frith's photographs can be seen framed and as giant wall murals in thousands of pubs, restaurants, hotels, banks, retail stores and other public buildings throughout the country. In every case they enhance the unique local atmosphere of the places they depict and provide reminders of gentler days in an increasingly busy and frenetic world.

Product Promotions

Frith products are used by many major companies to promote the sales of their own products or to reinforce their own history and heritage. Frith promotions have been used by Hovis bread, Courage beers, Scots Porage Oats, Colman's mustard, Cadbury's foods, Mellow Birds coffee, Dunhill pipe tobacco, Guinness, and Bulmer's Cider.

Genealogy and Family History

As the interest in family history and roots grows world-wide, more and more people are turning to Frith's photographs of Great Britain for images of the towns, villages and streets where their ancestors lived; and, of course, photographs of the churches and chapels where their ancestors were christened, married and buried are an essential part of every genealogy tree and family album.

Frith Products

All Frith photographs are available Framed or just as Mounted Prints and Posters (size 23 x 16 inches). These may be ordered from the address below. From time to time other products - Address Books, Calendars, Table Mats, etc - are available.

The Internet

Already twenty thousand Frith photographs can be viewed and purchased on the internet through the Frith websites and a myriad of partner sites.

For more detailed information on Frith companies and products, look at these sites:

www.francisfrith.co.uk
www.francisfrith.com
(for North American visitors)

See the complete list of Frith Books at:

www.francisfrith.co.uk

This web site is regularly updated with the latest list of publications from the Frith Book Company. If you wish to buy books relating to another part of the country that your local bookshop does not stock, you may purchase on-line.

For further information, trade, or author enquiries please contact us at the address below:
The Francis Frith Collection, Frith's Barn, Teffont, Salisbury, Wiltshire, England SP3 5QP.
Tel: +44 (0)1722 716 376 Fax: +44 (0)1722 716 881 Email: sales@francisfrith.co.uk

See Frith books on the internet www.francisfrith.co.uk

TO RECEIVE YOUR FREE MOUNTED PRINT

Mounted Print
Overall size 14 x 11 inches

Cut out this Voucher and return it with your remittance for £1.95 to cover postage and handling, to UK addresses. For overseas addresses please include £4.00 post and handling. Choose any photograph included in this book. Your SEPIA print will be A4 in size, and mounted in a cream mount with burgundy rule line, overall size 14 x 11 inches.

Order additional Mounted Prints at HALF PRICE (only £7.49 each*)

If there are further pictures you would like to order, possibly as gifts for friends and family, purchase them at half price (no additional postage and handling required).

Have your Mounted Prints framed*

For an additional £14.95 per print you can have your chosen Mounted Print framed in an elegant polished wood and gilt moulding, overall size 16 x 13 inches (no additional postage and handling required).

---

* IMPORTANT!
These special prices are only available if ordered using the original voucher on this page (no copies permitted) and at the same time as your free Mounted Print, for delivery to the same address

---

Frith Collectors' Guild

From time to time we publish a magazine of news and stories about Frith photographs and further special offers of Frith products. If you would like 12 months FREE membership, please return this form.

Send completed forms to:
The Francis Frith Collection, Frith's Barn, Teffont, Salisbury, Wiltshire SP3 5QP

Voucher for FREE and Reduced Price Frith Prints

Picture no.	Page number	Qty	Mounted @ £7.49	Framed + £14.95	Total Cost
		1	**Free of charge***	£	£
			£7.49	£	£
			£7.49	£	£
			£7.49	£	£
			£7.49	£	£
			£7.49	£	£

Please allow 28 days for delivery	*** Post & handling**	**£1.95**
Book Title	**Total Order Cost**	**£**

Please do not photocopy this voucher. Only the original is valid, so please cut it out and return it to us.

I enclose a cheque / postal order for £ . . . . made payable to 'The Francis Frith Collection'
OR please debit my Mastercard / Visa / Switch / Amex card *(credit cards please on all overseas orders)*

Number . . . .

Issue No(Switch only) . . . . .Valid from (Amex/Switch) . . . .

Expires . . . . Signature . . . .

Name Mr/Mrs/Ms . . . .

Address . . . .

. . . .

. . . . Postcode . . . .

Daytime Tel No . . . .   Valid to 31/12/02

The Francis Frith Collectors' Guild

Please enrol me as a member for 12 months free of charge.

Name Mr/Mrs/Ms . . . .

Address . . . .

. . . .

. . . .

. . . . Postcode . . . .

Would you like to find out more about Francis Frith?

We have recently recruited some entertaining speakers who are happy to visit local groups, clubs and societies to give an illustrated talk documenting Frith's travels and photographs. If you are a member of such a group and are interested in hosting a presentation, we would love to hear from you.

Our speakers bring with them a small selection of our local town and county books, together with sample prints. They are happy to take orders. A small proportion of the order value is donated to the group who have hosted the presentation. The talks are therefore an excellent way of fundraising for small groups and societies.

Can you help us with information about any of the Frith photographs in this book?

We are gradually compiling an historical record for each of the photographs in the Frith archive. It is always fascinating to find out the names of the people shown in the pictures, as well as insights into the shops, buildings and other features depicted.

If you recognize anyone in the photographs in this book, or if you have information not already included in the author's caption, do let us know. We would love to hear from you, and will try to publish it in future books or articles.

Our production team

Frith books are produced by a small dedicated team at offices in the converted Grade II listed 18th-century barn at Teffont near Salisbury, illustrated above. Most have worked with the Frith Collection for many years. All have in common one quality: they have a passion for the Frith Collection. The team is constantly expanding, but currently includes:

Jason Buck, John Buck, Douglas Burns, Heather Crisp, Isobel Hall, Rob Hames, Hazel Heaton, Peter Horne, James Kinnear, Tina Leary, Hannah Marsh, Eliza Sackett, Terence Sackett, Sandra Sanger, Shelley Tolcher, Susanna Walker, Clive Wathen and Jenny Wathen.